Get Up, Sam!

by Cameron Macintosh

illustrated by Dan Widdowson

OXFORD
UNIVERSITY PRESS
AUSTRALIA & NEW ZEALAND

Sam is sick. Sam is sad.

Mum got the duck.

Dad got the rocket.

Sam did not pick up the rocket.

Mum ran to get the sock.

Sam did not pick up the sock.

Dad ran to get Peg.
Peg ran to Sam.

Sam got up to pat Peg.

Sam is not sad!